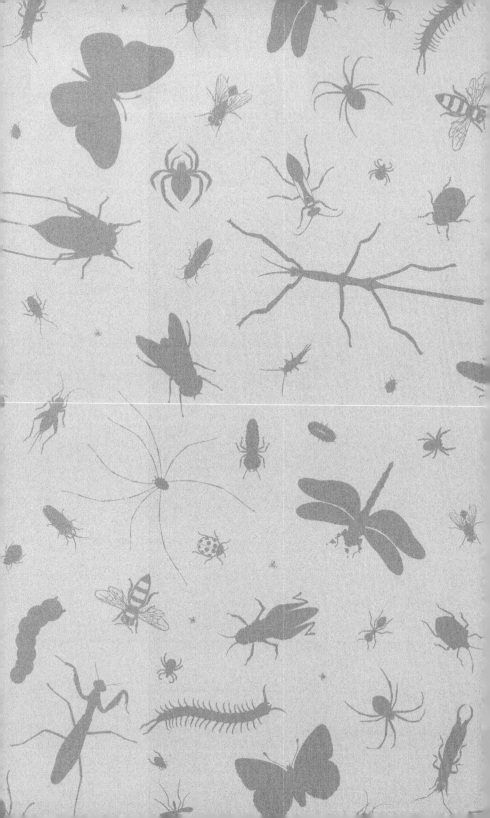

Special thanks to my wife and biggest fan,
Mindy, for her undying love, and endless
support and encouragement.

Thanks to my editor, Stacy Radil-Downs,
reading specialist, Dawn Manlove,
and beta reader, Sarah Gold,
for their meticulous attention to detail.

This is a work of fiction based on some real events, and involving real institutions. Names and characters are the products of the author's imagination. Any resemblance to actual persons, living or dead, is coincidental.

McC PUBLISHING
A part of Bright Ideas Graphics
ISBN: 978-0-578-98706-4

Copyright © 2021 Mark C. Collins

All rights reserved. No part of this book may be reproduced or transmitted in any form or by any means whatsoever without express written permission from the author, except in the case of brief quotations embodied in critical articles and reviews.

For those who enjoy the company of the creepy, crawly, many-legged little creatures of our planet.

Chapter 1
BUG BOY

"Bug Boy! Bug Boy! Heeeeyy... *BUG BOY!"*

Yep, that's me. Well, that's what my classmates and a couple of my fifth grade teachers call me. At home, even my dad sometimes calls me Bug Boy. My real name is Devin, but I admit, Bug Boy is a fitting title that I wear rather proudly.

They call me Bug Boy because I absolutely love bugs! I'm obsessed with them. Six legs, eight legs or dozens more... winged, wingless... stingers, pincers... insects, spiders; it doesn't matter. If it's creepy-crawly, I'm all in!

You won't find me on the swings, the jungle gym, or the monkey bars during recess. I rarely join a game of tag, or any other playground games. No sir! You'll find me on the school lawn, or along the fence under the row of oak trees, turning over rocks and nature's debris, looking for BUGS! With a bug jar in hand, I'm searching for new bugs, weird bugs; ones I've never seen before.

After four years of obsessive bug hunting, you'd probably figure that I've encountered nearly every type of bug in our region. But that's one of the wonderful things about the bug world; there's always more to discover!

Bug hunting is a solo activity. None of my friends or family ever care to join in. But that's totally cool with me. I'm a loner, but I'm never lonely. Bugs are my companions, despite how some people feel about them. Sure, there are quite a few pests in the bug kingdom, causing disease, property damage, and destroying food crops... things like that. But that doesn't mean *all* bugs are bad. Bugs just do what they do; what nature intended. We humans occupy *their* world. They were here first, and they outnumber us by astronomical proportions! They'll probably be here long after we're gone, too.

That said, it's not my intention to kill and keep the bugs I find, like some sort of mad scientist who collects bug corpses. I merely catch them, always handling them with care, place them into my bug jar, and observe their physical characteristics and behavior. I'll then look them up in one of the many bug books in my collection, take a few notes in my bug journal, make a sketch or two, then release the bug back where I found it.

Most of the bugs I've found are common to this region in southern New Jersey, and are easily referenced in an encyclopedia or on the internet. I've come across specimens of these common species many times in my daily hunts. There have been a few I've found that are *not* so common, and I'm always excited to study these first-finds, knowing I'll probably not come across another one like it anytime soon.

It was always a dream of mine to discover a truly new bug species; a bug never seen by humans before. And as rare as some of my finds have been, they never turned out to be the "undiscovered" species I had hoped for... until I made an amazing discovery just two weeks ago!

Read on, and I'll tell you all about it. But let's start at the beginning.

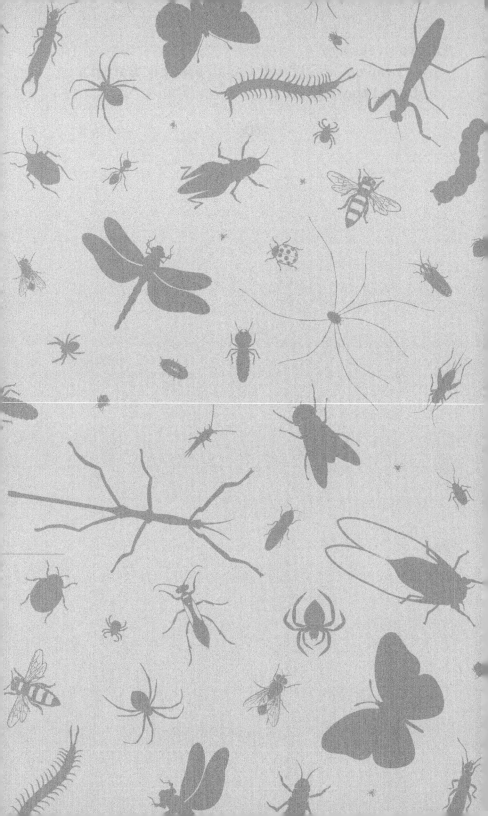

Chapter 2
AWAKENING

My bug obsession began when I was six years old. It was a hot summer Saturday afternoon, as I remember it. The cicadas were buzzing incessantly in the trees, though at that time I had no idea what that sound was. Mom was lounging on the front porch, sipping iced tea and reading a book. Dad was in the front yard weeding the flowerbeds.

I was busy making chalk drawings of rockets on our driveway, when I spotted a huge swarm of tiny brown ants that had gathered on the sidewalk. There must have been a thousand of them! My first reaction had been to crush them under my sneaker. Doesn't every little kid want to do such things?

A closer look stopped me, as I observed that the ants were engaged in a group effort of carrying a large, dead bug of some kind toward an open crack in the sidewalk. I was transfixed by their activity, and sat there watching them for what felt like an hour, as they eventually managed to accomplish their goal of bringing dinner home to the colony.

Dad even took a break from his weeding, curious as to what I was focused on, and joined me in sitting and watching this fascinating spectacle.

"What do we have here, Dev?"

"Ants, Dad. Hundreds of them! Hey Mom, come check this out!"

Mom cringed. She would have none of it and stayed safely on the porch. Bugs of any kind creep her out.

Dad and I watched until the dead bug had disappeared into the crack in the sidewalk, and the swarm of ants had dwindled in number to a few stragglers.

"Now that's what I'd call *teamwork*," Dad said.

From then on, I was hooked. I had suddenly realized that there was an entire world of life I had not previously considered – tiny creatures, each with a purpose and reason for existing, inhabiting the ground, air, water, and sometimes our homes – that was just begging to be studied, and I was ready to dig in!

DID YOU KNOW?

All bugs are arthropods. Arthropods are invertebrates, and have segmented legs and exoskeletons.

Invertebrate means without a backbone, or spine.

Exoskeleton means the bug has its skeleton on the outside of its body.

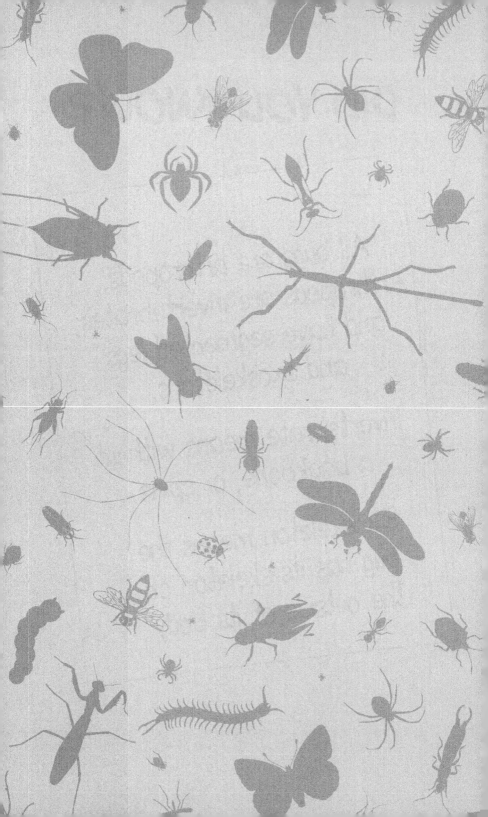

Chapter 3
PET

My initiation into this new obsession began a week or so later, when by chance I spotted a strange, scary-looking, slow moving bug on Mom's hydrangea bush in our backyard. This bug had an inch-long gray body, black spindly legs, and a long, curved, black needle coming from its face that extended beneath its body.

I went inside and fetched an old cardboard shoebox from my bedroom closet. Knowing the bug would need air, I poked a few small holes into the box top with a sharp pencil, and headed back outdoors, carrying the box.

Fortunately, the bug hadn't moved from the leaf it had been resting on before I went indoors. I filled the floor of the box with grass clippings and a few dead leaves. I wanted the bug to feel at home. Using a twig, I carefully knocked the bug from the bush into the box. I placed the top on the box and carried it to the picnic table on our patio.

The bug was now my very first pet! Of course I had no idea what kind of bug it was, or what it ate. At that time, I didn't even consider such things; only that I loved bugs and this weird one was now in my possession. I knew Mom would never allow it in the house, so I was forced to keep it outside in its cardboard home. I placed a small stone on the top of the box so the wind wouldn't blow the lid off overnight.

The next morning I awoke, it was a beautiful sunny day, but I noticed that it had rained during the night. I ran downstairs, past my mom, and out the backdoor, still in my pajamas. Everything on the patio was wet, and the cardboard box was so soggy, it looked like it had melted. The lid was off to the side, some of the grass was on the picnic table, and the stone ended up inside the box.

I looked for the bug, but it was gone! It had probably escaped during the night, taking advantage of the flattened shoebox walls. I was a little disappointed; not so much that the bug was gone, but that I hadn't thought it through enough to realize that a glass jar may have been more suitable for outdoor use.

In the end, it was probably best that I didn't get involved with that bug. I found out much later that it had been an assassin bug, a potentially dangerous insect with a painful bite that can cause sickness. It gives me the willies to imagine being poked by its needle-like beak!

I tossed the stone into the garden, gathered up the soggy shoebox, dumped it into the garbage can beside the house, and went indoors.

"Good morning, Devin. What were you doing outside in your pajamas?"

"Oh... good morning, Mom. You don't even want to know. But hey, do you have an empty jar I can borrow?"

DID YOU KNOW?

The three parts of an insect are the head, thorax, and abdomen.

Bugs don't breathe through their mouths. They breathe through holes called spiracles in their exoskeletons.

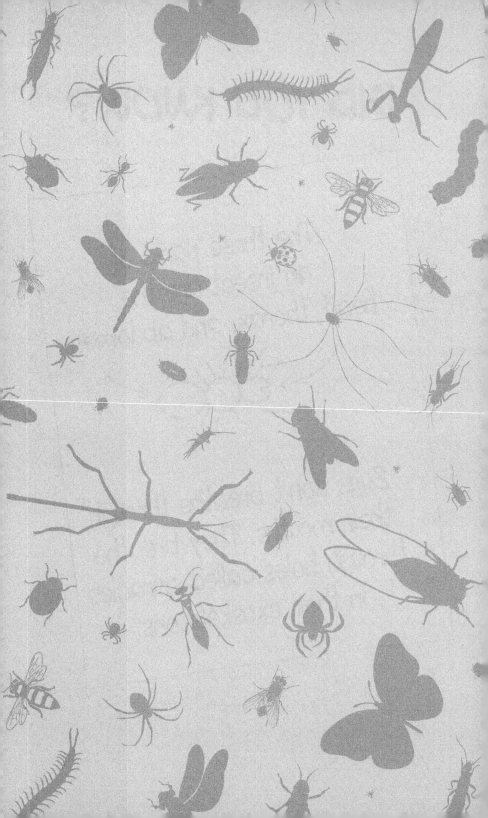

Chapter 4
QUEST

That first "summer of *bug* love" was filled with days where I spent most of my time hunting and interacting with bugs in our backyard and the small wooded lot next door. Even though Mom had given me an empty mayonnaise jar, I hardly used it as I originally intended because Mom would not allow me to bring any of my "pets" into the house. So, I gave up the idea of keeping bugs as pets, and instead made it a point to really understand each bug I found, through immediate observation. The jar became my "observation" lab.

By summer's end I had become casually familiar with the most common insects and spiders in our yard, though I didn't know the official names of many of them. We didn't have a home computer at that time, and I hadn't yet gotten my hands on a bug book of any kind, so I really couldn't do any research on the bugs I had found. I just enjoyed the interaction with them, and making drawings from my observations.

One of my favorite interactions was with tiny little "bees" that enjoyed landing on me and tasting my skin! They're the cutest darned things! Dad called them sweat bees. I found out later that Dad was wrong; they're not bees at all. They're really called hover flies; fearless yet harmless little flies with black and yellow-striped abdomens. Certainly nature had given them those defensive stripes to trick predators into thinking the hover fly was a stinging insect! Hover flies don't bite or sting, but love licking your skin for the salt that's in your sweat.

Jumping spiders were another favorite. They're too cute to be afraid of, and their quirky, inquisitive nature makes them appear playful. I've spent many hours "playing" with them. They seem to enjoy a session of hide and seek with my fingers. I've never been bitten by a jumping spider, and don't know anyone who has.

Many of the other bugs I frequently encountered included ladybugs, crickets, various beetles (my favorite was the click beetle, which, when it found itself on its back could turn itself upright with a click of its head), fireflies (we called them lightning bugs), grasshoppers, stink bugs, various spiders, daddy-long-legs (which look like spiders, but aren't, although they are cousins), butterflies, moths (and caterpillars), and of course pests like houseflies, mosquitoes, and the dreaded tick.

Most all of the non-pests ended up as drawings in my little sketchbook, while pests like mosquitoes and a few ticks attacked me all summer, like little blood-sucking vampires!

DID YOU KNOW?

A larva is the young stage of a bug's life. Caterpillars are the larvae of butterflies and moths. Maggots are the larvae of flies.

Most insects go through 4 life stages: egg, larva, pupa, and adult.

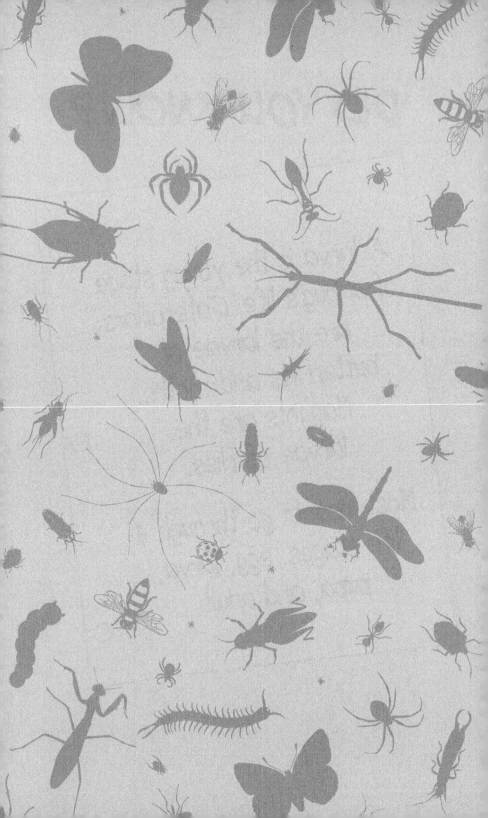

Chapter 5
NOISY TREES

For as long as I can remember, nearly every summer day was punctuated by an odd, loud buzzing sound high up in the trees. In fact, if I didn't have a calendar, and nobody told me what time of the year it was, I would still have known when summer arrived by the noisy trees!

"That sound comes from locusts," Dad told me.

I had no idea what locusts were. It wasn't until I became a bug enthusiast that I discovered how wrong my dad was! Locusts are actually grasshoppers, and grasshoppers don't make buzzing sounds like that.

The real noisemakers are called cicadas. Cicadas are very large flying insects that start their lives underground as larvae. Each summer they mature to adulthood, come up out of the ground and climb up the trunks of trees. There, they shed their skin (called molting), climb into the upper branches to suck the juices of trees and make that incessant buzzing sound.

You've probably found their brown, crispy shells stuck to the trunks of trees and wooden fences. I've found these shells many times, but have only rarely seen the bug itself. They're very strange looking... kind of scary at first, with big, bulging eyes and a needle-like proboscis (a tubular mouthpart similar to a drinking straw). But cicadas are generally harmless. They don't defensively bite or sting, but if you hold one, it might think you're a tree and try to suck juices from your hand with its proboscis.

Cicadas make that particular sound to attract a mate. The sound comes from special organs inside their bodies. Sometimes the sound is so loud it can be heard a mile away! Another amazing fact is that cicadas can live from four to 17 years, depending on the species. Most of that time is spent underground as larvae. Cicadas only live a couple of weeks as mature adults up in the trees.

As if it's not bad enough that cicadas live such short adult lives, there's a type of wasp that *kills* cicadas. It's called a cicada killer (as if it was a challenge for whoever came up with that name). These cicada killers are huge and scary looking, like hornets! They're not usually aggressive toward humans, but they attack cicadas, sting them repeatedly, and take the paralyzed cicada back to the cicada killer's underground nest to feed its larvae. I witnessed an attack happen one time in our backyard.

I was on our patio, when out of nowhere a cicada fell from the sky just a couple of feet in front of me. I jumped back, startled, and noticed the cicada had a cicada killer on its back! The wasp kept stinging the poor cicada, but the cicada continued crawling along the patio and up a tree trunk, struggling to escape. I lost sight of them as they disappeared into the leaves of the tree. I'm pretty sure the cicada didn't get away that day, and some cicada killer larvae got a nice cicada meal of crunchy wings, legs, and bulgy eyes for dinner!

DID YOU KNOW?

Most insects molt as they grow. Molting means they shed their hard exoskeleton, which doesn't grow with them. Underneath is a new exoskeleton that's very soft, but hardens over time. When they outgrow this layer, they molt again, up to 6 times until adulthood.

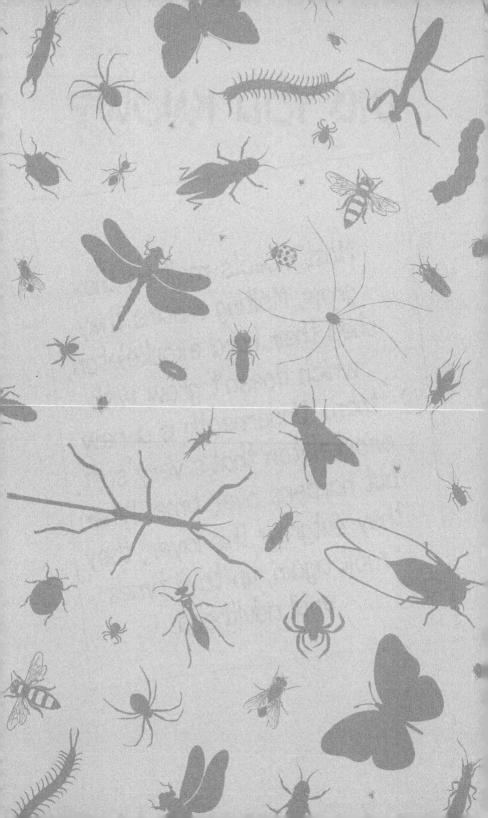

Chapter 6
ANTVENTURES

Since ants were some of the most common and numerous insects in our yard, I'd play around with them most frequently. I had no need for the mayonnaise jar with ants because I could observe so many of them at once in their natural settings.

There were large black ants, medium-sized red ants, and tiny little brown ants. These species usually avoided contact with the others, and each species behaved a bit differently than their cousins.

Black ants and red ants could be aggressive if handled, so I usually kept my attention on the harmless tiny brown ants. I often watched as they followed one another in long lines on the sidewalk, or up the side of our house. I loved diverting their direction with a swipe of my finger across their trails, and watch them act all confused, walking in circles or zigzagging, trying to find the trail and their friends again. I learned later that ants follow each other by scent.

Other times I'd use a magnifying glass and send a hot beam of laser-like sunlight down on them, just to watch them run away like crazy! Sure, it was cruel, but I don't do things like that now that I'm older and wiser. At the time, I thought it was fun.

The thing I did with ants most often was capture them and drop them into spider webs found in the corners of our garage, then wait for the spider to come out of its web tunnel. I'd watch in amazement as the spider would run out, take a quick bite of the ant, then swiftly spin a thread around the ant until it looked like a tiny mummy lying on the web.

The spider would often retreat back into its web tunnel, evidently saving the ant as a meal for later.

I can't even tell you how many times I had done this over those summer months and the following two years! Countless ants became meals for hungry spiders because of me, "Chef Devin!"

DID YOU KNOW?

Ants are the longest living insects.

Ants don't have ears.

Ants can lift 10-50 times their body weight.

There are one million ants for every human on our planet.

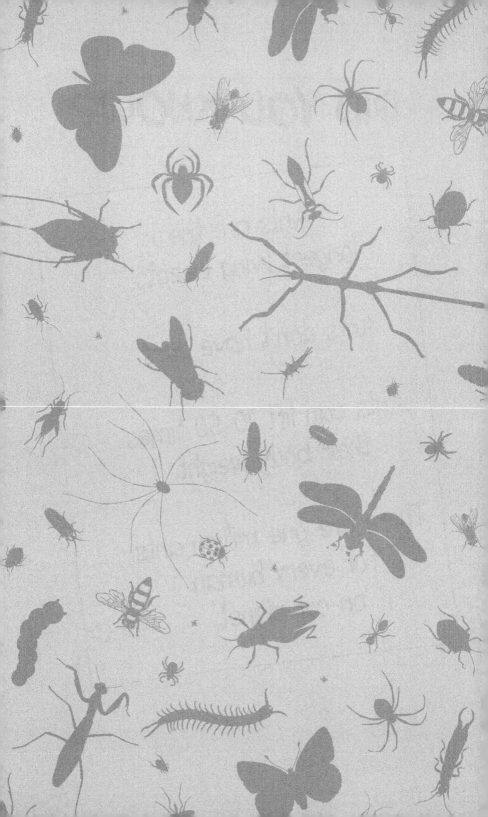

Chapter 7
BATTLE BUTT

I loved turning over rocks, leaves, rotting tree bark; any type of yard debris that might uncover some new bug. Usually I'd find the very common, gray, pill bug, which is often more commonly called "roly-poly" due to the fact that it rolls up into a ball when touched or frightened.

Pill bugs gather in little groups under rocks and in dark, moist areas, and when uncovered, will scatter. They're harmless little dudes, and seem more like they belong in the sea, which isn't surprising when you consider that they're not insects at all. They're crustaceans, and related to crabs and shrimp! In fact they're the only crustaceans that live their entire lives on land.

Another common bug found in dark, moist areas is the earwig. Yeah, it's a creepy name for a bug, and if you've never seen one, it's like something out of the imagination. It's got a longish, rather common-looking, dark brown body, but has a set of pincers on its *butt!*

Years ago, many people falsely believed that earwigs could crawl into the ears of sleeping victims and lay their eggs in the victim's brain! This is probably the reason the earwig got its name. Even today many folks are frightened of earwigs (even if they really don't believe the egg-laying part), and assume that the pincers can harm you.

Well, I can tell you from experience this is not true. I've handled earwigs countless times, and although they certainly can pinch you if they feel threatened, the pinch doesn't break the skin or even hurt. Earwigs use their pincers to defend themselves from other bugs. Can you imagine being bug-sized, confronting and battling an earwig? Yikes!

DID YOU KNOW?

Pill bugs are crustaceans, breathe through gills, and live in moist environments, but they cannot survive under water.

There are 2,000 species of earwigs, found on every continent except Antarctica.

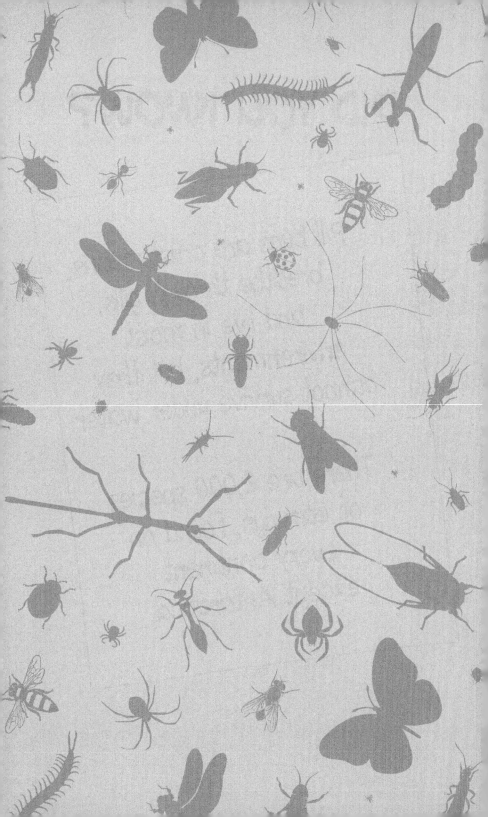

Chapter 8
GLADIATORS

My mom had a large terrarium where she grew beautiful tropical houseplants in at one time. Eventually the plants died and so the terrarium sat, unused, on a shelf in the garage for the previous couple of years. It was simply a large, shallow, yellow bowl topped with a large, removable, clear plastic dome that had a small hole at the top. All that was left in the terrarium was dried up soil. I had been thinking about turning it into some kind of bug habitat, but could never decide what bugs to choose, or how to set it up. So there it sat, useless on the shelf.

Early one evening as the sun was going down, I spotted a large, dark brown wolf spider crossing the path in front of our shed. Fortunately, I had my mayonnaise jar in hand and carefully captured that spider by placing the opening of the jar in the spider's path, and nudging the spider along with a quick, light tap of my fingertip until the spider entered the jar. I suddenly remembered the empty terrarium in the garage and ran to dump the spider into it. This darned terrarium would get some use as a spider home after all! As long as I didn't bring it into the house, Mom shouldn't have a problem with whatever I put into the terrarium.

I watched the spider inside the terrarium, slowly circling the perimeter of the bowl. The spider looked bored to me. I returned to the yard to look for small stones, branches, some moss; whatever I could find that would contribute to making a suitable habitat for a bored wolf spider. I picked up a nice big piece of curved bark on the ground that had fallen off the sycamore tree along our neighbor's fence. I jumped back, startled from what was beneath. I couldn't believe it; another large, brown wolf spider that looked like the other's twin!

Using the mayonnaise jar, I quickly captured spider number two and headed for the garage again. I dumped the spider into the terrarium's hole and watched as it landed on the soil below. The first spider would now have a friend. I went back outside to fetch items that would make the terrarium feel more like nature. Then it dawned on me; how will I get the items into the terrarium? Placing sticks, stones, plants, and other larger items would require that I remove the large dome from the big bowl at the bottom. Once the dome was removed, the spiders would escape, and let me tell you, wolf spiders are fast. Really fast!

I went back inside the garage and stood there, staring blankly through the big dome, thinking about how I could solve this problem. The obvious solution would have been to furnish the interior of the terrarium before adding the spiders!

Suddenly the spiders themselves distracted me. They walked in the same direction around the edge of the terrarium, but across from each other as if trying to avoid confrontation.

I didn't know it at that time, but most spiders are

solitary beings and do not like the company of other spiders. Wolf spiders are great hunters and don't use webs to catch prey. They simply hunt down their meals and quickly grab them.

It became apparent to me that these wolfies might not like each other! At that point, I no longer cared about making a home for them. I was simply fascinated by only watching them and wondering how they might interact with each other. I had no idea how this situation would play out.

The spiders continued walking in the same direction around the dish, keeping a safe distance from each other at opposite sides of the bowl. One would be a little faster than the other, bump into the rear of the slower one, which made the slower one suddenly speed up. This continued for a spell until they both just stopped walking altogether. They rested at opposite sides of the terrarium. I waited and waited some more.

My impatience got the better of me and I tapped the side of the plastic dome, jolting one of the spiders into action. Having resumed his walk, he reached the opposite side of the dish and rear-ended the other spider (who suddenly resumed his walking), and quickly changed direction. Now both spiders walked in opposite directions and appeared to be on an eventual collision course! My heartbeat sped up as the distance between the spiders shortened with each step they took toward each other. They stopped walking within two inches from one another, and stood motionless for several seconds. Perhaps each spider sensed danger from the other, through scent or sight, and avoided contact.

I pondered this momentarily when suddenly they

lurched forward and clashed in a death clutch! My heart seemed to skip a beat in nervous excitement. The spiders were locked together like two small hands with fingers tightly intertwined. I watched as the losing spider fell prey to the victor's bite; the loser's brown body covered in tiny white droplets oozing from its pores as the venom of the victor took the life out of the loser.

I felt kind of sick to my stomach, and a little guilty for setting the whole thing in motion that resulted in the death of a big, beautiful spider... all for my entertainment and morbid curiosity. I told myself I'd never again pit one spider against another, like gladiators in the Roman Colosseum.

Disgusted with myself, I carried the terrarium out to the yard. I placed it on the ground beside the fence, removed the dome, and went up to my room for the night. When I returned the next day, the spiders were gone. I replaced the dome on top of the bowl, and returned the empty terrarium to its shelf in the garage, where it sits, unused to this day.

DID YOU KNOW?

Spiders aren't insects. They're arachnids, along with other eight-legged creatures like ticks and scorpions.

The poison from a black widow spider is 15 times deadlier than a rattlesnake's.

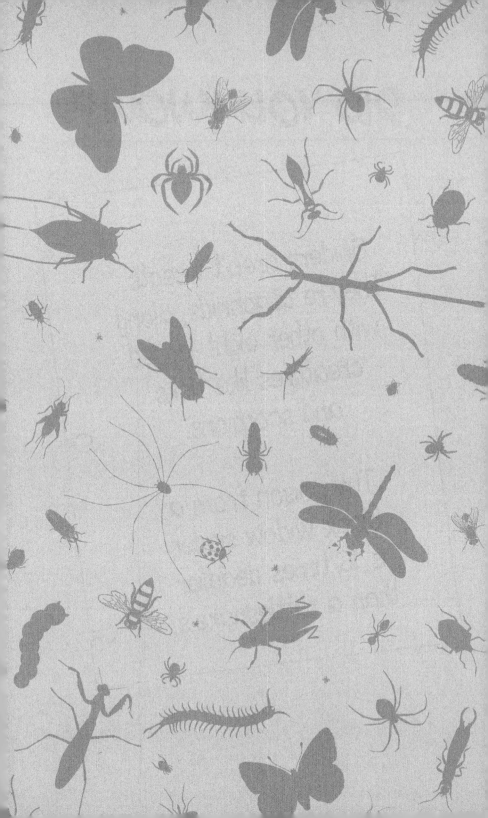

Chapter 9
A THOUSAND LEGS

I really have no fear of most bugs. I'm fully aware of the danger some bugs might present, and I respond accordingly. In most cases, it's just a matter of respecting them and not acting in a threatening manner when encountering one. Or better yet, just plain stay away from them. I'm talking about bugs like wasps, hornets, some ants, and certain spiders. Even the praying mantis can do some harm if threatened. In other words, leave *them* alone, and they'll do the same with you.

That said, there is one type of bug that creeps me out more than any others; the centipede! Especially the house centipede. Perhaps it's because they have so many legs that stick straight out, or maybe because they move so swiftly and can crawl into the tiniest of cracks and crevices. Yuck... I'm getting freaked out just describing them!

If you've never seen one, this probably won't sound so frightening. At first glance (and if it's sitting still), the house centipede looks kind of like a feather. Non-threatening. But just go ahead and disturb it! That thing will swiftly shimmy away, all its legs moving in a rhythmic pattern, until it finds a tiny hiding place to squeeze into. So, even after all these years of being exposed to countless bug species, I'm still hesitant to handle a centipede. Avoiding them, not handling them is just fine with me.

Oh, did I mention that they might bite? Well, it's more like a pinch. The centipede uses two hollow legs near its head to pinch and inject poison. That's probably another good reason to leave them to their business, which is catching other bugs that are pests in the house!

Now the millipede, the centipede's cousin, is a different story. I have no fear of those little buggers! Millipedes are thinner, move slower, and although they have many legs, they're *tiny* legs that are set beneath its body. If you touch a millipede, they kind of curl up in fear! Millipedes don't bite, but they will secrete a defensive substance that has a peculiar, pungent scent if you handle one.

By the way, centipedes and millipedes aren't insects at all. They're in a family called Myriapods. Isn't the bug world amazing?

DID YOU KNOW?

Some centipede species glow in the dark.

Some centipede species can live as long as 6 years.

Millipedes were the first animals to live on land.

"Millipede" means 1,000 feet, but most millipedes have fewer than 100 feet.

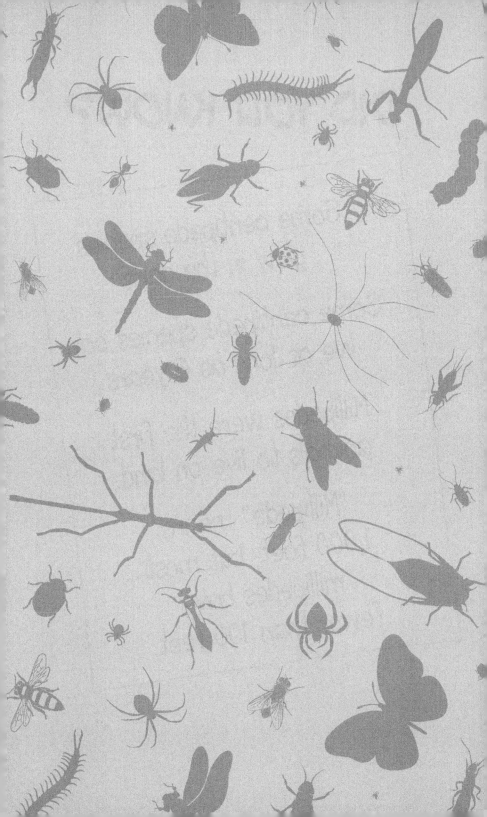

Chapter 10
GIFTS

As summer turned to fall that year, school started and the weather got colder. That meant most bugs disappeared and my bug hunting had to stop until spring when warmer weather would resume. Mom occasionally called on me to remove a spider from the house (killing it was never an option), but that was pretty much my only bug interaction every winter.

So, when not doing homework, drawing, or completing one of my chores, I spent most of my free time at home looking at the few bug books from the school library. The books were so old and didn't include certain bugs and up-to-date facts. We didn't yet have a home computer back then, so the internet was no help for me. I complained to Mom about it.

"We can try the public library in town and see if they have any newer, more up-to-date bug books," replied Mom.

Thanks Mom!

Well, we never went. And it wouldn't be long before I found out why.

My seventh birthday came that December. Mom planned a small, bug-themed party and said I could invite some school friends. Steve, Randy, and Clifford were there, as well as my grandparents and my cousin Herbie.

Mom decorated a cake with plastic toy bugs. It was deliciously gross looking! Or would that be grossly delicious-looking? Anyway, I blew out the candles and made a wish.

I had only been into my bug obsession for a few months at that point, so I wasn't yet known as "Bug Boy" at school. My friends brought gifts unrelated to my bug obsession. Steve gave me a model World War 2 airplane. Randy brought a 500-piece puzzle of the moon landing, and Clifford gave me a word game called "Boggle." These were really cool gifts, but I was so bug-obsessed, I didn't appreciate their gifts at the time, even though I acted like I loved them.

"Thanks fellas!"

Then I opened cousin Herbie's gift. An ant farm!

"I hope you like it, Devin. I have one just like it at home and it's fun to watch the ants live and work in the ant farm."

"Thanks Cuz!"

Up next were gifts Mom and Dad had gotten me. I tore off the wrapper, jumped up and exclaimed, "AL-RIIIIGHT!" My birthday wish came true with an official BUG JAR! Now I could recycle that old mayonnaise jar. This pro bug jar had a vented lid, and a magnifying glass built right into its side! I could easily observe any bug in it, up close! The second gift was a journal in which to sketch and jot down notes about the bugs I would catch and observe.

"Thanks Mom and Dad!"

Then it was onto a heavy gift from my grandparents. I could barely lift it toward me on the table. All I could imagine was that they had packaged up a stack of bricks as some cruel joke on me! I tore off the wrapping paper and in my complete surprise, I just stared, open-mouthed at a stack of... new and up-to-date BUG BOOKS! There was a huge hardback encyclopedia of insects and spiders. This thing was nearly three inches thick! It would take me all of first grade and well into third grade just to get through it! There were also a dozen smaller paperbacks of particular species like bees, ants, and dragonflies.

"Wow, thanks Mom-mom and Pop-pop! How'd you know I like bugs?"

"Grandparents just know these things, Devin," Mom-mom said.

Now I was ready. I had all I really needed to up my game in studying the bugs I'd find. I couldn't wait to get started! But it would have to wait until spring.

DID YOU KNOW?

Ticks can grow to the size of a marble.

Houseflies live for one month.

Dragonflies have the highest hunting success rate of any predators on earth.

A caterpillar has more muscles in its body than a human does.

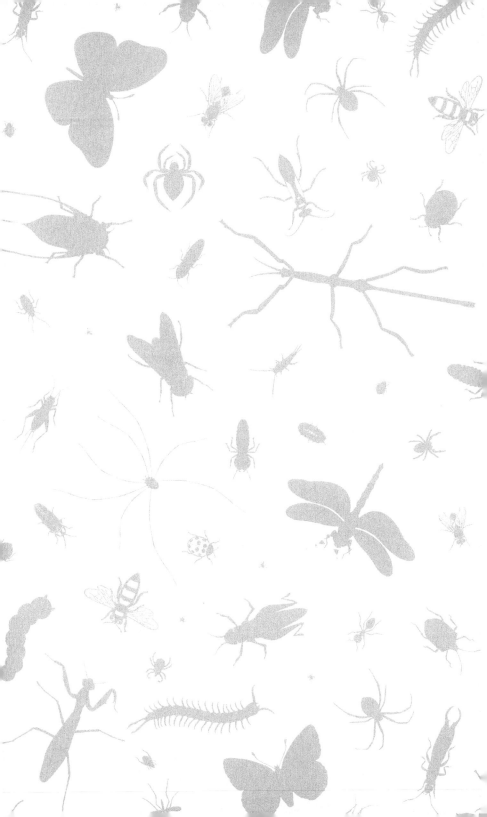

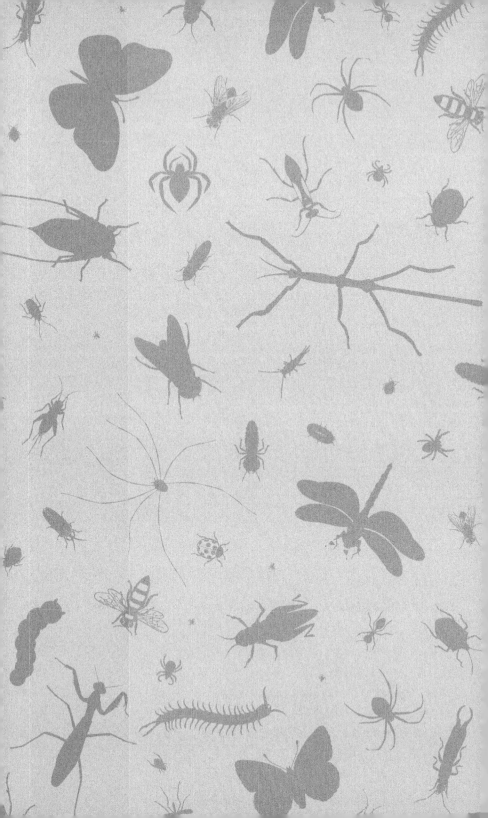

Chapter 11
BACKYARD BUZZ

When I finally turned 10 last December, Dad informed me that one of my chores for spring was mowing the lawn. I don't mind mowing the grass. In fact, I do a darn good job! However, if I wait too long between mowings, not only does the grass get tall and harder to cut, but clovers and dandelions sprout little white and yellow flowers all over the yard... which mean one thing; honeybees! I love honeybees, so if they're all over the flowers when I mow the grass, I become their unwitting executioner!

Cutting the lawn should normally take an hour, but when bees are present, I mow very slowly, trying not to run over a single bee! They're usually so focused on their work collecting nectar, they don't realize the danger coming up on them. It sometimes takes me two hours to finish mowing when I'm trying to avoid mowing over the little buzzers. I love bees that much!

Mom tells me that when I was a toddler, I accidentally stepped on bees many times when I ran around barefoot, resulting in painful stings and a lot of tears. I don't remember stepping on them, but I do recall being three years old, seeing a honeybee on a dandelion flower in our backyard and thinking how cute she looked, all fuzzy and dusted with pollen. Impulsively,

I reached out with a finger and tried to pet her on her back.

Annoyed, she flew off to another flower and I followed, intent on petting her again. But she would have none of that! Thinking that I was a threat, she stung the tip of my index finger! I burst out crying from the pain of the sting as the little bee flew away. Mom came running out of the house into the yard.

"What's wrong? What happened?"

"I touched a bee and it stung me!"

I calmed down after Mom took hold of my hand and carefully removed the stinger by pinching it between her fingernails.

"You know, you shouldn't touch honeybees, Devin. When they sting, they lose their stinger and they *die*."

I felt so bad that the little bee was going to die that I began sobbing again. Mom took me inside. She said that a freshly sliced onion placed on the sting for a few minutes would take away the pain. Now I don't know if that's really true, but that smelly onion brought even *more* tears to my already-watery eyes!

That day, I learned a lesson to never touch another stinging insect directly again. Well, up until I turned eight. I had figured out how to touch honeybees without getting stung. It's really all in how gentle you are. Honeybees aren't as aggressive as yellowjackets, wasps, and hornets. In fact, honeybees don't really want to sting if they don't have to. They're usually too busy being busy... as bees! Thank goodness for that! Without bees and the essential pollination they do, we would have no food. And definitely, no honey!

DID YOU KNOW?

A bee's wings beat 190 times per second. That's 11,400 times a minute.

Only female bees can sting. Male bees don't have stingers.

Bees have existed for around 30 million years.

SPRING

Chapter 12
EAT PREY, LOVE

One day I spotted a beautiful, huge praying mantis in the foliage of one of the small trees along our driveway. There's no way I was going to put *that* one into a bug jar! I already knew that mantids were predators that ate other bugs, and I wanted to witness that with my own eyes. But the mantis just stood there on the branch, not moving. There were no other bugs around him that could have ended up as his lunch. So I had an idea.

I ran to the garage where I often encountered shiny, black field crickets that scattered when the light came on. Well, I had no problem finding one! It had a back leg missing and was unable to hop away under the utility shelves where they often hid. I gently scooped it up with my hand and ran back outside to the tree.

The mantis was still there, motionless as before. I lifted the cricket by its single back leg and held it a couple of inches in front of the mantis. The cricket began to squiggle a bit. The mantis lifted its head, obviously observing the cricket with its big eyes. Then, in a swift motion that made me jump, the mantis reached out with its front leg pincers and grabbed the cricket from my hand! I watched as the mantis ate the cricket alive! The crunchy sound it made as the mantis bit off pieces of the cricket and chewed them up just added to my viewing experience.

I was amazed at how quickly the mantis had completely devoured that entire cricket! I've come to love mantids more than any other bug, and always look forward to seeing the tiny baby mantises all over the bushes in our yard each spring.

DID YOU KNOW?

The praying mantis has 3D vision, but can't hear very well.

Some praying mantises can fly.

The praying mantis is the only insect that can turn its head and look behind its back.

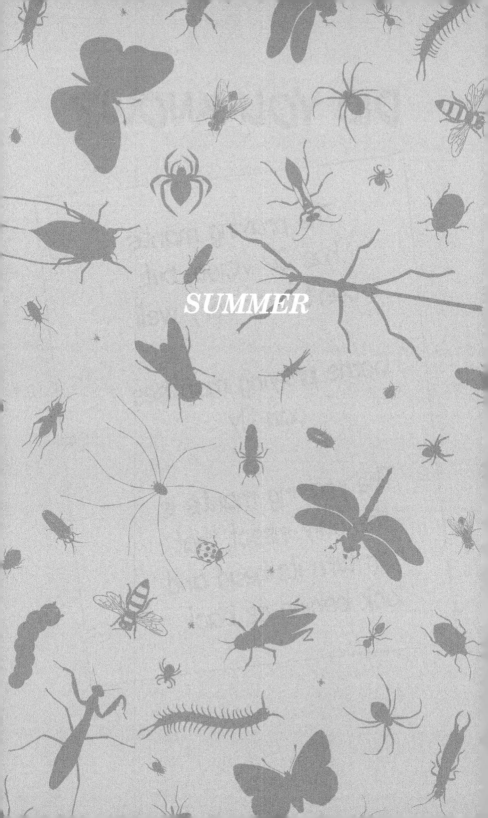

Chapter 13
SQUIRMING RICE

Like every other kid, I love summer vacation; not only as a 3-month long break from school, but because it allows me more time to — you guessed it — seek out and study bugs!

The other great thing about summer vacation is; the weekend after school lets out, Mom, Dad, and I pack up the car (including my bug jar and a few bug books) and head down to the beach for the whole summer! Two years ago, Dad bought a little house on the bay in Delaware, and there's wetland, forest, and bay beach — all within walking distance... which meant I got to spend hours looking for coastline bugs on days we all didn't go to the beach. Sure, the greenhead flies, gnats, and mosquitoes dive-bombed me on my first outing in the wetlands and along the woods; their bites resulting in itchy welts. But I can get by pretty well now on my bug hunts if I wear bug repellant and long sleeves.

Most of the bugs I encountered were nothing unusual. Water striders, dragonflies (which my dad would always refer to as "snake doctors," so named in the old-fashioned false belief that dragonflies repair injured snakes), mayflies, crane flies (which look like giant mosquitoes, but are harmless), and waterbugs —

just to name a few of the outdoor varieties. Indoors I'd find silverfish (not a fish at all), millipedes, and house spiders. Mom always recruited me to remove them for her, of course.

A walk along the bay beach sometimes turns up a variety of carcasses; dead sea creatures in various states of decay. The common horseshoe crab that patrols the shallow water along the bay shore often gets stranded as the tide subsides, and ends up dying on the sand in the hot sun. This is where bugs begin nature's clean-up chores!

All too often I'd come across a beached horseshoe crab. In my effort to rescue it, pick it up to return it to the water, I'd realize that it was not only dead, but infested with maggots underneath!

If you didn't already know, maggots are white, worm-like fly larvae. Flies lay their eggs on dead things and when the eggs hatch, the maggots emerge. Maggots will eat up all the soft parts of a carcass, and bacteria do the rest until there's nothing left of the dead animal but bones or shell.

As disgusting as that sounds, it's a benefit in nature. Imagine if we had no maggots for the clean-up task. There would be dead things lying around, piled up everywhere. Imagine trying to walk around all those dead dinosaur carcasses!

Well, I had never seen maggots before our first time coming to the shore. During my first encounter, I thought the maggots were white rice that somehow ended up all over a dead fish I had found on the bay beach. Then I noticed the rice was squirming! Let me tell you, once you see something like that, you'll never look at a plate of chicken-fried rice in the same way again!

DID YOU KNOW?

Maggots are sometimes used medically, to eat away dead flesh in a person's wound. This helps the wound heal faster.

Every year a person probably eats about one pound of flies, maggots and other bugs without even knowing it.

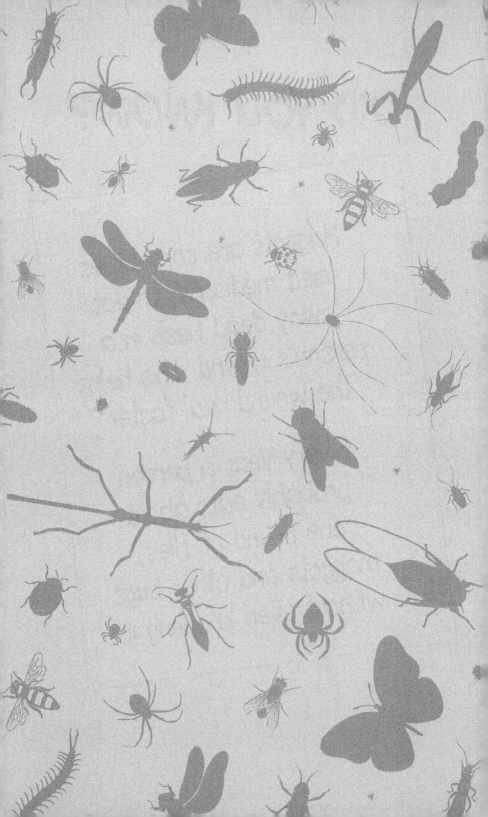

Chapter 14
ALIEN SPIDERS

My first chore when we arrive at the shore house is to turn on the water supply and electricity to the house. Each had been turned off during the winter when we're away and no one occupies the house. The water valve and electric switch are located in a tiny, low-ceiling, cinderblock shed on the edge of the property.

The very first time Dad assigned me this chore, he told me where the valve and switch would be within the shed, explained how to turn them on, and told me that it was *my* job because the shed is too small and cramped for him to easily get in to get the job done. My dad isn't a large man, so I had a suspicion that wasn't the real reason, but I agreed and made my way into the shed, as Dad helped Mom unpack the car.

I opened the shed door and stood for a moment to let my eyes adjust to the darkness within. Dad was right; it was cramped in there. I bent forward and stepped into the unit and encountered a few spider webs across the space. No big deal. I don't mind spiders, especially the spindly, harmless, common house spiders that occupy spaces like basements or the interior of a shed.

I wiped the webs from my face and shoulders,

and moved inward toward the back of the shed where the valve and switch were. A beam of sunlight came through the doorway just as I caught a glimpse... of a HUGE spider, like nothing my eyes have ever witnessed! It clung to the wall to my left. I froze in fear and noticed the entire floor near the back of the shed, and halfway up its walls were covered in this same type of alien-looking spider. There were dozens of them, in many different sizes. My hair stood on end!

I took a deep breath and reached slightly forward toward the water valve on the back wall near the floor, trying not to step on any of the spiders, when suddenly one of the large spiders *jumped* directly at ME! This created a domino effect and within seconds *all* of those alien spiders began jumping, bouncing off walls and ME! I ran screaming out of the shed, frantically brushing off any spider that may have clung to my shorts and shirt.

Mom became alarmed and shrieked, "What's wrong? What is it?"

Dad just stood there by the car's open trunk, luggage in hand, laughing his head off.

"Cricket attack, son?"

"No, Dad... SPIDERS!"

"I think you'd better go back and have a closer look," he said.

I curiously, yet cautiously went back inside the shed. The commotion had calmed down and I took a closer look. Indeed, these were not spiders after all, but strange crickets that were completely foreign to me.

After turning on the water and power to the house, I retrieved the bug jar from my backpack in the house, and returned to the shed.

It took a few tries, but I managed to catch one of the largest crickets. Once inside the jar, the cricket jumped so radically and violently against the jar's walls that I feared it might tear itself apart. It eventually calmed down enough that I was able to observe its strange features and look it up in my bug encyclopedia.

What an awesome specimen! It turned out to be a cave cricket (sometimes called a camel cricket), common to the region, dwelling in basements and cave-like environments. The cave cricket has a shorter body than most other cricket species, and it curves upward in a kind of hump — sort of like a shrimp's body does. Its legs splay outward like a spider's legs do, which is the reason that I (and most people) initially confuse the cricket for a spider. Its back legs are very long, with the knee joint jutting upward. No wonder this thing jumps like a pro!

I thoughtfully jotted down the day's experience with the cave crickets in my journal, then released the cricket into the backyard.

Later that evening, during dinner, Dad apologized for sending me into the shed. He told me it was still my chore from now on if I wanted it, but he just wanted to be sure I wasn't too shaken up. I assured him I was fine, and that it actually was a great learning experience.

When Dad gathered the dirty dishes from the table and went into the kitchen to clean up, Mom leaned in to me and whispered.

"Do you want to know the *real* reason your father assigned you the water and electricity chores?"

"Yeah, Mom. Tell me!"

"Well, the very first time your dad went into that shed, he came running out screaming!"

DID YOU KNOW?

Camel crickets don't chirp, or have wings like other cricket species do.

Most crickets have wings, but do not fly.

A cricket's ears aren't on its head. They're on its front legs just below the knees.

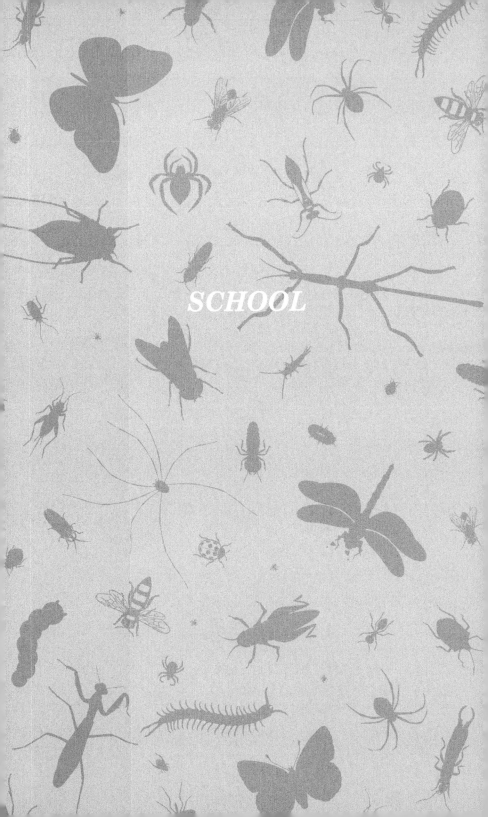
SCHOOL

Chapter 15
ART & ENTOMOLOGY

Did I mention that I'm a pretty good artist? That's right! Along with my love for studying bugs, I love drawing them! Actually, drawing was my very first love, and I wanted to be an artist for as long as I can remember. When bugs became my obsession, I suddenly had great subjects from which to draw. The variety; shapes, textures, and colors of the bugs were great challenges for me to capture on paper. My grandpa always jokes that I'm good at "drawing flies."

Anyway, I've spent much of my free time during the cold months indoors, copying photographs of bugs I found in books. I applied what I learned from our art teacher in school. Mr. Kuhn taught us about light and shadow, how to look at objects as basic shapes, and how to see the negative spaces around objects as objects themselves. I know that seems hard to understand, but once you grasp the concept, it really helps you become a better artist. And it really helped me see bugs in their proper form and to make accurate drawings of them.

I won two of our school's art shows with renderings of bugs I had made. My first show was won with a graphite pencil drawing of a wasp's face, really close-up, on a large sheet of white paper. I tried to make it as realistic as possible using shading and shadows. Every hair, every pore and bump were carefully observed and drawn. Even the compound eyes! It took me almost three weeks to complete the drawing.

I won my second art show with a drawing of a honeybee hovering over a daisy. The drawing was really cool, because I used a black colored pencil on a golden yellow sheet of paper, and drew all the highlights in with a white colored pencil. I didn't have to use a yellow colored pencil because the paper was yellow.

As good as I think I am at making art, my biggest competition at school is Lauren Bischoff. She does these amazing watercolor paintings of flowers with shiny, green leaves! They're so realistic-looking, you could almost *smell* them. I don't know how I managed to win shows when Laura was entered in them too. She's *that* good. Second place might mean she's only a point or two away from taking First place, so I had my work cut out for me to stay ahead.

In preparation for next year's art show in middle school, I've really been working hard, studying color theory, and making full color sketches. With that knowledge and practice, I plan on making a detailed colored pencil drawing of one of the most brilliantly-hued butterflies in existence; the Emerald Swallowtail! Of course I hope to win, but even if I end up in second place, I'll still come away a winner of sorts. There's always something to gain from learning something new.

Mr. Kuhn pulled me aside in art class one day.

"Hey Devin, have you thought about making a career in art when you grow up? Your bug drawings are excellent. You might consider being an entomological illustrator."

"I hadn't really thought about it, Mr. Kuhn, but it sounds like a great plan!"

I got really excited visualizing combining my two biggest loves from which to make a career. Getting paid to draw bugs for textbooks, museum exhibits, science and nature magazines sounded like the best job in the world! His words were so inspirational, and fired me up about both of my obsessions.

Drawing realistic bugs from nature or photographs is a fun challenge, but the real fun is drawing bugs from my imagination. I've created countless drawings of fantastical bugs, combining parts from many different real bugs, as well as making up my own weird bug parts. There are endless possibilities! What's really surprising is when I'd come up with an impressive-looking imaginary bug, only to find out later that there's already a bug species just like it that actually exists! Nature is so weird and surprising. It's true... sometimes reality is stranger than fiction!

DID YOU KNOW?

The study of arthropods is called arthropodology.

The study of insects is called entomology.

The study of myriapods is called myriapodology.

The study of arachnids is called arachnology.

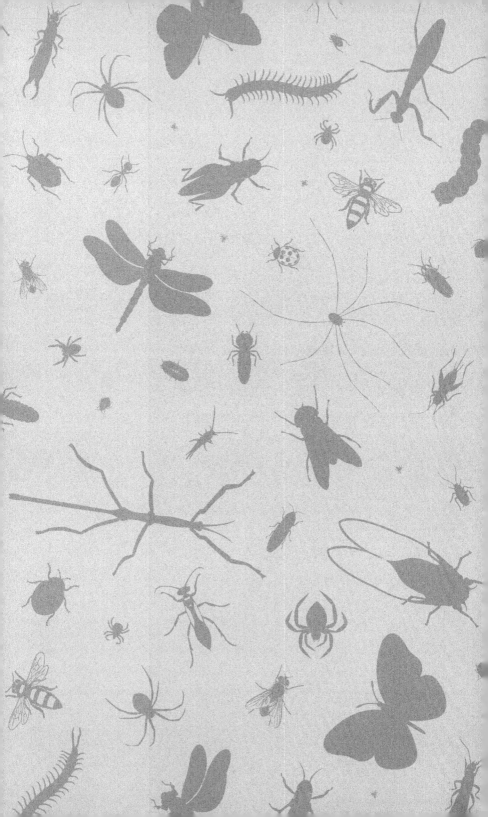

Chapter 16
PRANK

I have to admit; sometimes my bug-drawing obsession lands me in hot water. Figuratively, of course. Last semester, Mrs. Harrington our math teacher called my mom in for an after-school conference. You see, I usually finished my test papers before my classmates, then used the spare time to mindlessly draw bugs in the margins of my completed test papers (never mind that I always aced my tests). I didn't think drawing bugs on a test paper was a big deal, but Mrs. Harrington and my mom had a different opinion. Mom scolded me in the car on the way home.

"Math problems are for math tests. Bug drawings stay in your *sketchbook*. Understand, Devin?"

"Yes, Mom. I'm sorry."

Yet somehow her warning failed to influence my behavior; for a month later I pulled what I thought would be a hilarious prank on Mom.

She went next door to a neighbor's house one afternoon. I saw my chance, snuck into the laundry room, jumped up onto the clothes dryer, and drew a *huge*, realistic shiny black beetle on the wall, complete with a finely rendered drop shadow beneath the beetle. This thing had to be three inches long, and when I finished, it looked like a real, three-dimensional bug clinging to the wall, especially from a distance away. I laughed to myself almost the entire time I spent drawing the bug for my prank. I couldn't wait for the next laundry day to see Mom's reaction.

Well, days passed and I had forgotten about the drawing prank. Then, about a week later, I nearly jumped out of my skin when I heard a thump and my mom scream like I'd never heard before! I ran to see what the trouble was, and there was Mom, standing in the laundry room doorway, her hand over her mouth and the spilled laundry basket at her feet. She looked at me and slowly pointed into the room, above the dryer.

"THAT *BUG!* Did one of yours escape?"

I chuckled. "No, Mom! It's a drawing."

She looked at the drawing again, then back at me.

"Devin, what did I tell you?" Her voice darkened and got louder.

"Bugs stay in your sketchbook. *Do you understand me?"*

I nodded.

"Now go clean it off the wall!"

I spent twice as much time erasing and scrubbing that darned bug drawing off the wall than I had when putting it there in the first place. Even after all that work, I could still see a trace of the beetle on the wall.

I went to the garage, found a paintbrush and the can of off-white paint used once before in that room. A few strokes with the brush and paint did the trick. No evidence a drawing was ever there after that. I cleaned the brush and put everything away just as Dad came home for dinner. I was afraid Mom would tell him about my prank as we ate. Lucky for **me**, she didn't.

Later that night, after I finished brushing my teeth before bed, I heard Mom tell Dad all about the prank.

"You should have seen this thing, Greg. It was so *realistic* looking!"

I held my breath, fearing Dad might come bounding down the hall to scold me. Then I heard them both... *laugh!*

"That boy is so talented," Dad said.

"He sure is," Mom said. "Like an evil genius!"

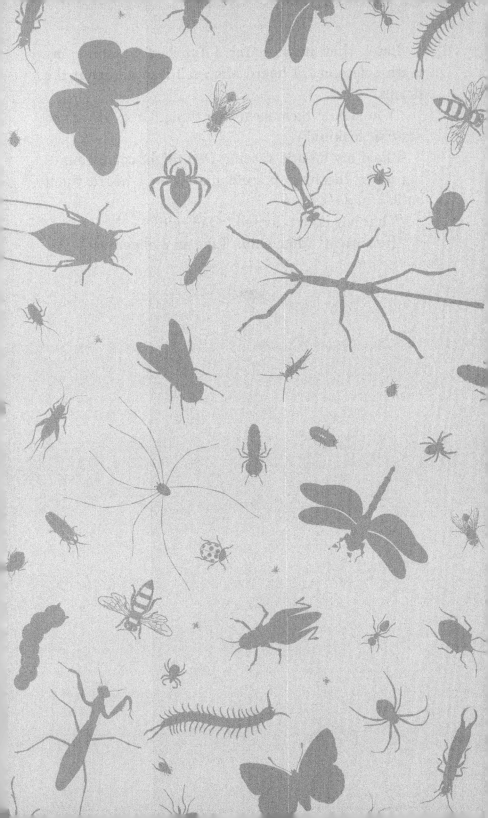

Chapter 17
METAMORPHOSIS

We read some pretty good novels over the course of this school year in Miss Banks' fifth grade English class. Ernest Hemingway's, *"The Old Man and the Sea,"* Gary Paulsen's, *"Hatchet,"* and *"The Outsiders,"* by S. E. Hinton; all of them had me glued to their pages for several nights each. Miss Banks said she was saving the best book for our last semester, but didn't reveal its title until late in May.

When we all filed into English class that Friday after lunch and took our seats, a paperback copy of this book sat on every desk. I picked up my copy to inspect the cover. There was a modern art-style illustration of a large beetle filling almost the entire cover; its spindly legs spread out to the edges. Their knobby joints and hairy lengths added a creepy tone to the illustration. Above the artwork, the title and author's name appeared; *"The Metamorphosis"* By Franz Kafka.

I had never heard of this Kafka dude, but then again I hadn't heard of the previous three books' authors either.

"Class, this is our final book of the year, and it's my all-time favorite," said Miss Banks. "Enjoy reading it, and be ready to discuss it in a week. I expect your essays the following Friday."

As Miss Banks began distributing our graded tests we took the previous week, I read the synopsis on the back cover of *"The Metamorphosis."* Very interesting! How could it *not* be? The main character in the story turns into a *bug!* A *real* bug boy! I couldn't wait to begin reading it that night.

I'm not going to spoil it for you by saying anything more about it. *"The Metamorphosis"* ended up being my favorite novel, and it could be yours, too. Read it and see why!

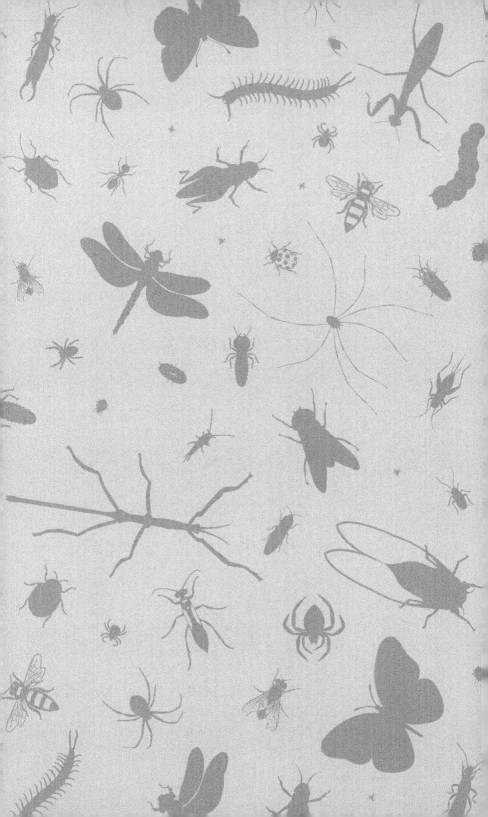

Chapter 18
VISITORS

Later that afternoon in science class, Mrs. Colby had a great surprise for us. We were studying the ecosystem (the study of all living things and how they relate to the environment), and Mrs. Colby had booked a guest speaker to visit our classroom to discuss a particular important element of the ecosystem. No one could guess which element. Shortly after, a man in a green jumpsuit strolled into the classroom pushing a handcart stacked with three large plastic crates.

"May I have everyone's attention?" Mrs. Colby announced. "I'd like to introduce you all to Dr. Alito. He has some interesting friends he'd like you to meet."

Friends?

"Maybe rats or snakes," whispered my lab-mate Bobby Moore, sounding hopeful. I just rolled my eyes.

"Good afternoon, class," our guest greeted. "As Mrs. Colby told you, I am Dr. Ronald Alito, but you can call me Ron."

He continued. "I'm here, visiting all the way from The Philadelphia Academy of Natural Sciences, and I'm an entomologist."

Did he just say entomologist? I couldn't believe it!

Dr. Alito then asked, "Does anyone know what an entomologist studies?"

No sooner had those words left Dr. Alito's mouth, my hand shot straight up.

"BUGS!" I blurted out, almost leaping from my seat. Some of the kids laughed.

"That's correct, young man. We study insects, and sometimes arachnids and other arthropods."

Ron went on to explain the differences between those groups, and the very important roles that species in each group played in the ecosystem. He also informed us that there are over a million arthropod species worldwide! That's far more species than any other group of living things on the earth!

He went on to reveal more interesting facts about bugs, many that I already knew due to my own study. The most amazing fact that I *didn't* already know was that scientists discover an average of three new insect species per week. *Per week!* He said he was sorry that he was unable to bring along any of those exotic new bugs, but he did have an impressive little collection that he was certain we'd all enjoy meeting. I couldn't wait!

First up was a stick insect named Ludwig. He looked exactly like a twig on a tree! When Ron asked the class for a volunteer, once again my hand involuntarily went straight up!

"Well, aren't you enthusiastic! What's your name, son?"

Before I could answer, one of the kids called out, *"Bug Boy,"* and the whole classroom broke into laughter... even Mrs. Colby!

"My name is Devin."

"Well, Devin, you obviously like arthropods! Come

on up and be my assistant."

Ron let Ludwig walk up my arm and onto my shoulder. Some of the kids exclaimed, "*Ew, gross!*" But I didn't mind. Ludwig was harmless. I knew from my own reading that stick bugs dwell within our region, but I had never been fortunate enough to encounter one. Maybe because stick insects are so well camouflaged, I couldn't see one that might have been right in front of me. It was fun meeting Ludwig.

I have to admit, *ew, gross* was my first thought when Ron brought out the next guest; a Madagascar hissing cockroach named Remy. And I mean this fella was HUGE! I was a little freaked out when Ron placed Remy onto the back of my hand! But I really had nothing to fear because cockroaches don't bite, and Ron said this one ate lettuce and carrots.

Remy didn't hiss at first, but when I touched his very shiny back with my other hand, he let out a quick hiss and his antennae twitched faster! It made me laugh, so I did it again... and the class laughed!
Remy crawled all over my hand and in between my fingers.

Ron said Remy was almost five years old! As Ron put Remy away, he advised that I wash my hands before eating later because even though hissing cockroaches are very clean insects, they might possibly carry mold spores that can cause an allergic reaction in the handler. Mrs. Colby was quick to provide the hand sanitizer!

Up next was Victor, a tarantula from the US Southwestern desert. Now I've come in contact with all kinds of spiders in our yard and nearby woods, but

I've never seen anything like the monster that Victor appeared to be. His fangs were nearly one inch long! I had no intention of holding this big fellow, so I was relieved when Ron made no mention of doing so.

Ron told the class that tarantulas could live up to 20 years! He also said that all spiders have a venomous bite when catching prey. However, Victor was well fed, and would not bite if handled carefully and with respect. Besides, tarantulas from the Southwestern USA aren't very aggressive and have relatively weak venom, so even if they did bite, despite being painful, the venom would be no worse than a bee sting... that is if you're not allergic to bee stings!

Ron held Victor in his palm, and Victor covered Ron's entire hand! Everyone got a chance to come up and gently pet Victor. Not everyone took that opportunity. Mrs. Colby kindly declined, although she did admit that Victor was quite an impressive specimen. I could tell by the look on her face that she was actually grossed out.

Ron finished up by telling us that some cultures eat tarantulas! That's right, people of Cambodia enjoy tarantulas... *FRIED!*

At the end of the seminar, everyone applauded as Ron packed up his bug pals.

"Thank you for assisting me today, Devin."

"I should be thanking YOU, Ron! I love bugs with a passion, and hope to be an entomological illustrator someday," I said, pointing to some of my bug drawings hanging over the lab sink.

"You're very talented," Ron said, adding that entomological illustration would be an admirable career.

"You should contact the academy when you're through your education and training when you grow up. Who knows if your talents might be needed there."

"You bet I will!"

We all said our goodbyes and Ron headed down the hall and out to his van with his bug cargo.

I sat there for a moment, fully inspired by his visit. Meeting his bug buddies was certainly a treat, but it was one thing in particular he had said that fired me up; that scientists discover an average of three new bug species per week! For as long as I have been passionate about bugs, that's the one thing that's become a life dream; discovering a new bug species, being known as its discoverer, and possibly being able to name it!

What a great ending to the school day! A book about a bug in English class, and real bug visitors in science class!

I did my homework on the bus ride home that afternoon. I planned on finishing my chores at home, then spending the rest of the day outside, looking harder than ever for new bugs!

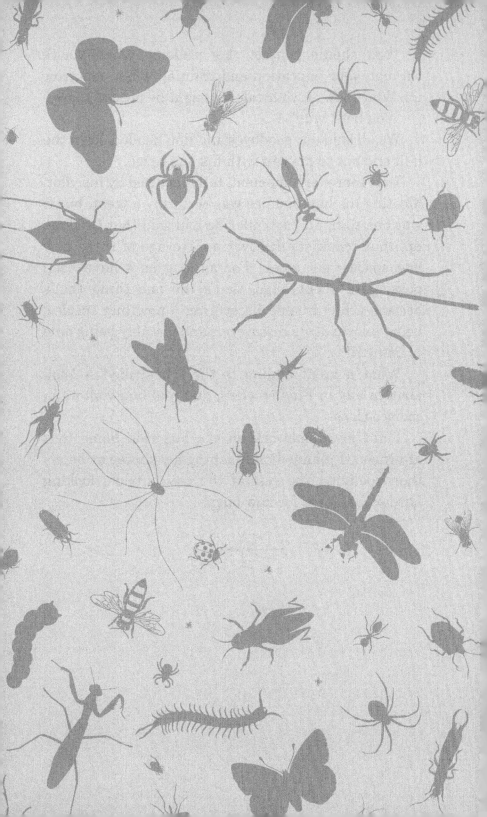

Chapter 19
THAT BUG!

After completing my homework on the bus, I returned my notebook to my backpack and took out my copy of *"The Metamorphosis"* that Miss Banks had handed out in English class earlier in the day. I read the first two pages and was so immersed in the story; I forgot that my stop was next! I quickly packed up and headed up front, ready to step off the bus.

We were in the final weeks of school, the weather was very warm, and all the kids were loud and rowdy with the anticipation of summer vacation to come. I exited the bus and headed up our driveway while a few kids yelled from the open windows as the bus pulled away.

"Bye-bye, Bug Boy!"

I laughed to myself and waved without looking back as I approached the mailbox by our front door. It was my job to bring in the mail every afternoon – a simple chore I enjoyed. Sometimes there was mail for me in the form of a nature magazine. It was extra special if the magazine had an article about bugs.

However, that day's mail collecting brought an unexpected guest! Just as I reached for the mailbox lid, a tiny mantis-like ant stood on the lid and reached out its front legs toward my hand! *What is THIS?*

I knew from experience that ants do not react in such a way. This thing obviously had terrific eyesight in order to see me coming, and to react by reaching out to me!

I fearlessly, yet carefully offered my index finger to this tiny creature, which climbed up on it, seemingly as curious of me as I was of it! I brought my bug-inhabited finger up to my face for a closer look. It reminded me of some of the imaginary "Frankenstein" bugs I draw in my sketchbook; using parts from different bugs to create a new one.

This bug was similar in body shape and color to a red ant, but had "arms" with pincers at the end like those of a mantis! It also had a stinger, and a set of segmented antennae that twitched rapidly. I had never seen anything quite like this before, neither in life, or any bug books.

Could this be a new species yet undiscovered? Could this be what I have been waiting for these past few years of obsessive bug hunting and research?

Why not? I couldn't wait to find out. Kafka would have to wait until tomorrow!

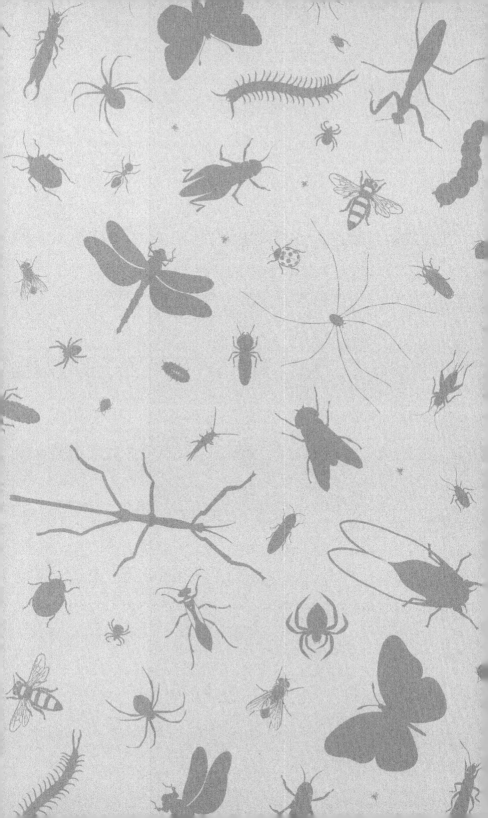

Chapter 20
TWITCHY

I collected the day's mail and went inside, mail in one hand, and my new little friend clinging to my finger of the other hand. Mom raised a suspicious eyebrow when she saw me with my small cargo. I knew she didn't want any bugs in the house, especially one so strange and seemingly unpredictable.

"Mom, I know what you're thinking, but I think this is the one! You know... what I've been dreaming about? A truly rare find!"

She certainly knew by the look on my face, and acknowledged.

"I'll go get your bug jar," she said, taking the mail from my hand and hurrying up to my room to fetch the jar.

"You can keep it in the house just this once, Devin," she said when she returned with my jar.

Once my little twitchy buddy was safely inside the jar, I went back outside and carefully added tiny twigs, and some small leaves to the jar. I splashed a few drops of water inside as well, and replaced the lid. At least this tiny creature would be hydrated until I could figure out what it ate.

I ran upstairs with the jar and took off my backpack. I set the jar on my desk and turned on the lamp.

The built-in magnification of the jar's side made the little bug look much bigger than it actually was, and I was able to define each part quite easily. I opened my sketchbook and drew the new bug as faithfully as possible. I then pulled out all my bug books (a collection that now included more than 20 books on arthropods) and went through each one, using a bit of logic in determining which category this bug might fall into. Was it an ant, or a mantis? Or was it something completely different and new?

An hour passed and I still found nothing related. At first I became frustrated. *I'm a good researcher! Why couldn't I find this little bugger in these books?* Then it dawned on me again.

Hold on, Dev, it's probably not in the books because it's RARE or UNDISCOVERED! On the other hand, perhaps my books were already outdated. They *were* a few years old by then.

I ran downstairs and asked Mom if she'd take me to the bookstore.

"After dinner, Dev. Let's see if your father wants to go, too."

I've always loved going to the bookstore with my parents. Every time we go, we separate and disappear into our favorite sections. I go to the nature and bugs section, or the art section. Dad goes to the history or sports sections, and Mom goes to the romance or interior decorating sections.

After dinner we all got into the car and Dad drove into town. I even brought the bug jar along so I could compare the little bug with what I might find in the books at the bookstore. I did get a few strange looks from some of the customers in the store.

We spent almost two hours there, until closing. Good thing it was a Friday night! Unfortunately, none of the new books there had anything referencing the little bug in my possession. I had to keep reminding myself that it was a good thing! It only reinforced my belief that this was a true, rare find!

By the time we got home, I was exhausted. I felt brain-dead, yet oddly exhilarated by the thought that this could be the bug I had been waiting for all along. All those hours, adding up to days, weeks, months, perhaps even years of hunting for that one rare, undiscovered bug. Now, here it was, almost as if all my effort had manifested this moment!

I placed the jar with Twitchy (yes, that's what I named him, due to his twitchy antennae) on my nightstand, switched off the light, and plopped into bed, too tired to change my clothes or brush my teeth. I drifted off to sleep and dreamed of weird bugs all night long.

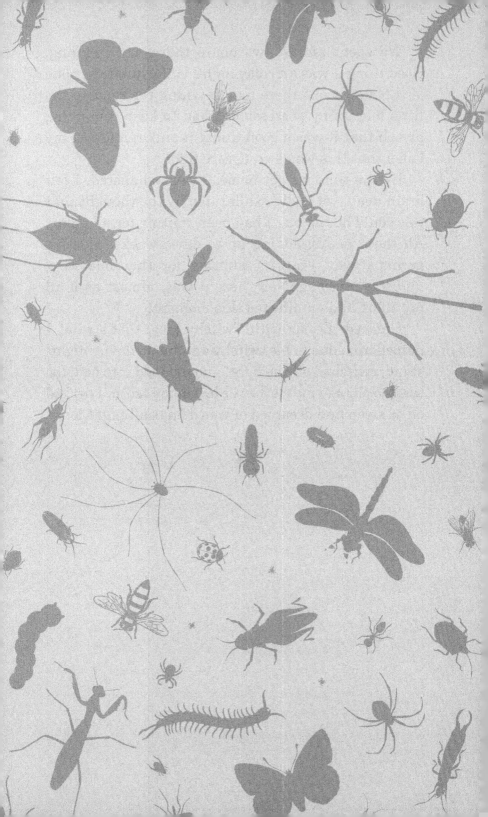

Chapter 21
THE ACADEMY

The roar of Dad's lawnmower yanked me out of a deep sleep. It was *my* chore, so why was Dad mowing the lawn, and why so early on a Saturday morning?
I looked at the clock and noted that it wasn't so early after all. It was almost noon! I couldn't remember the last time I woke up *that* late, and still wearing the clothes from the day before.

I got up, grabbed the bug jar, and headed downstairs for breakfast. A stack of cold pancakes awaited me on the table. Mom had made them before she went out Saturday shopping.

I sat eating while I observed Twitchy's actions, and contemplated my next move. *How can I find out about the origins of this odd little bug?*

I heard the lawnmower shut off outside, and a moment later my dad walked in, sweating.

"Oh, there you are, sport. Did you have a good night's sleep?"

"It was like I was in a coma, Dad!"

"Yeah, I know," he said, pouring himself a tall glass of iced tea.

"I tried waking you up, but you were so out of it I decided to just let you rest."

"Thanks Dad! Need any help out there today?"

"Nah. I got this one. You can resume it next weekend," he replied, gulping down his drink and putting the empty glass into the sink. He glanced back at me as he headed out the door.

"Enjoy your day, *Bug Boy!*"

My day? Oh yeah... my next move. I finished my breakfast and sat there just staring blankly into the direction of the breakfast nook, when it came into focus; *Mom's computer!* Of course! Why hadn't I thought of that before! She had only recently gotten the laptop, so it wasn't something I was used to using regularly. Now I had the internet and the potential of finding my bug online. Thank goodness for modern technology!

After cleaning up the breakfast dishes, I raced upstairs, brushed my teeth, changed clothes, and headed back down to the kitchen. With bug jar beside me at the table, I sat for the next hour or so searching the *web* (hah, notice the pun?) and every bug-related website I could find. Nothing!

I finally decided to be less species-specific, and typed in *"entomology"* as a search. A list of entries popped up. My eyes scrolled down the list, and there, under one of the headings within the descriptive paragraph was a name that just seemed to jump out at me; RONALD ALITO! I couldn't believe it! I clicked the entry and saw that it was a career bio for an entomologist from the Philadelphia Academy of Natural Sciences — the very same guy who visited our school just the day before! Of course Ron would know what to do about Twitchy!

I found the phone number, called the museum and asked for Dr. Alito. The receptionist on the other end asked me what the call was about.

"Just please tell him that it's Bug Boy, from the school he visited yesterday."

She laughed.

"Okay, I'll tell him. Hold please."

Twitchy was walking upside down on a leaf as I glanced into the jar, on hold, waiting for Ron to pick up the phone.

"I'm going to find out about you yet, little buddy! And if not, then I'm your discoverer for sure!"

There was a click on the line.

"Well, hello Bug Boy! This is Ron. How are you doing this afternoon?"

"I couldn't be better, Ron! In fact, I have something you might be interested in!"

I went on a lengthy explanation of my discovery, describing in full detail every aspect of what I observed in Twitchy. Ron thought the name was funny, and was extremely interested in this little critter. He offered to do some research for me... and Twitchy.

"Can you email pictures of Twitchy to me?"

"Sure! When my mom gets home, I'll use her smart phone to take a few pictures, then I'll send them to you."

"Great! I look forward to getting them."

I carefully jotted down his email address as he recited it.

"I'll contact you in a few days with what I find. Have a nice weekend, Devin."

"You too, Ron! Talk to you soon!"

I nearly jumped for joy when I hung up the phone. I could be days away from entomological fame and notoriety! *I'll bet no one my age is discovering new bug species!*

Mom got home a short while later. I helped put away all the groceries while I explained everything to her.

"Oh, I hope it all goes as you hope, Dev!"

I took many photographs from different angles and close-ups using Mom's phone. Although Twitchy was rather tiny, he looked HUGE in the photos.

I used Mom's phone to forward the photos, along with our home phone number, to Ron's email address. Ron replied a few minutes later, and once again reminded me that he'd get back to me in a few days. Now all I could do was wait.

Heck, what are a few days? I can wait, and I'm sure Twitchy will be fine until then. Then it hit me; I didn't know what Twitchy ate in nature, so I had no idea what to put into the jar. *Hopefully he won't starve in the next few days!*

I took that time to read *"The Metamorphosis,"* and wow, Miss Banks was right! What a story! Funny, yet strange and sadly tragic all at once. I finished it in one night, and took the next few nights to conceive and write my essay. At least I was productive in order to keep my impatience from getting the better of me while waiting for Ron's call.

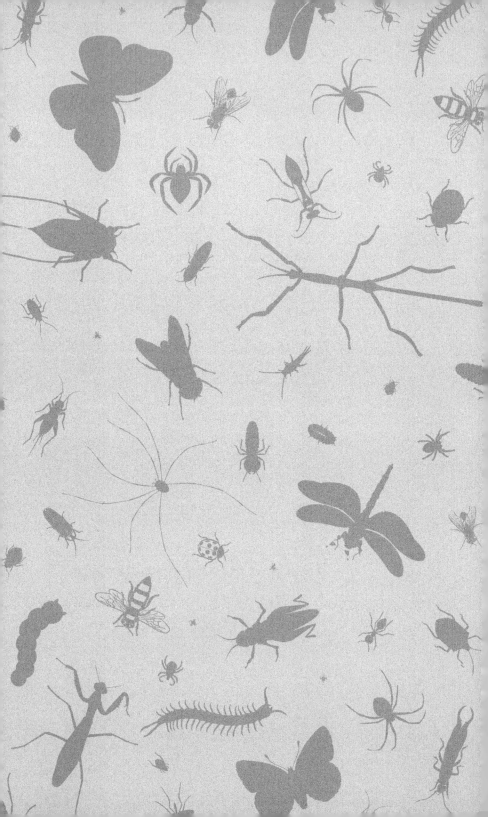

Chapter 22
THE CALL

Days passed. More than a few. In fact, a whole week had gone by! I couldn't believe Twitchy was still alive, but I wondered how much longer he could go without eating. It didn't look like any of the fresh leaves I put into the jar had been chewed on. I never kept any bug in the jar *that* long.

I began thinking that perhaps Ron forgot about me, or maybe he was just too busy at the museum to research my bug. Then I allowed a selfishly unfair thought to enter my brain; what if Ron found out that Twitchy was indeed a new species and *he* took the credit as its discoverer, instead of me?

I jumped... startled when the phone rang. I bolted downstairs, just hoping it was Ron, and also hoping I could answer the phone in time before he hung up.

"Hello, Devin speaking," I said, catching my breath.

"Hi Devin! It's Ron."

I breathed a deep sigh of relief. Ron must have heard it because he sincerely apologized for the long delay in getting back to me.

"Well, Devin, I hope I don't disappoint you, but your bug is not a new, previously undiscovered species."

I sighed. "Oh well..."

"Hold on, Dev. It's still good news. Not only is your bug a rare find, it's *extremely* rare!"

Ron continued, saying that only two specimens of this particular species had been discovered previously, and that both were found in *Hawaii*.

"That's thousands of miles away," I exclaimed, and wondered how this one got all the way to the east coast of the continental United States.

Ron went on to tell me the name of this bug, which wasn't an ant or a mantis after all! It was actually a wingless wasp called a *Dryinidae*. He said there are over 1,400 known species of this type of wasp, and that it's a solitary wasp, which means it doesn't live with other wasps in a hive. Dryinidae wasps also happen to be *parasitic!*

"What you thought was a stinger, is actually an ovipositor, which the wasp uses to inject eggs into the body of an insect host, namely leafhoppers. You see, the wasp uses her mantis-like front legs and pincers to grab her prey before depositing her eggs inside the host's body. When the eggs hatch, the larvae eat the body of the living host from the inside out until the host dies, and the larvae become adult wasps."

"That's disgusting... *and* incredible! But wait... are you telling me that Twitchy is actually a female?"

"Yep. In fact, so were the other two that had been found in Hawaii. Males have never been found, but we assume they would be like other varieties of Dryinidae wasps, in that they'd look different than the females, have wings, but no ovipositor, obviously."

I sat speechless for a moment, digesting everything Ron had just explained. My disappointment in not discovering an unknown species was replaced by the wonder of all the facts on this strange little wasp.

"Hey Devin, I'd love it if we could add Twitchy to the Academy's collection. Any chance you can bring her here?"

"Sure, but I'll have to ask my mom to drive me there."

"Whatever you can do. The museum closes at 5 o'clock today. When you arrive, just go to the front desk and ask for me. I'll see you when you get here. Have a safe trip, Devin!"

He hung up and I turned to Twitchy.

"You're gonna be in a museum, little girl!"

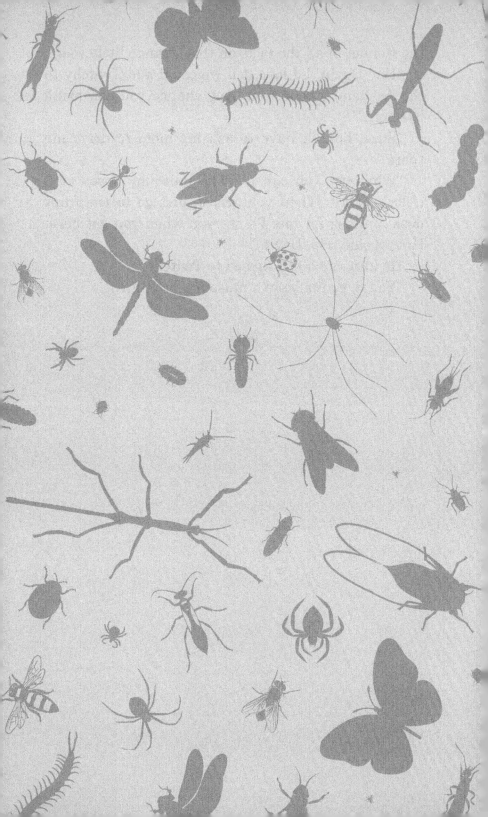

Chapter 23
TRAFFIC JAM

Mom agreed to drive Twitchy and me into the city to The Philadelphia Academy of Natural Sciences, where Ron awaited my arrival. I didn't want to leave my bug jar there, so I had to transfer Twitchy to a disposable container. Mom found an old baby food jar that was perfect. I could run inside the museum and just hand off the jar with Twitchy inside, and leave before the museum closed at 5:00 pm. I checked the kitchen clock. We had about an hour to get there. Surely, traffic into Philadelphia wouldn't be so bad on a Saturday afternoon.

Boy, was I wrong! The roads from our house were clear, but by the time we crossed the Betsy Ross Bridge and swung down the ramp onto Interstate 95, we had to merge into bumper-to-bumper traffic. The cars were crawling slower than a slug in syrup!

"I wonder what's causing all this traffic," Mom said.

"I just hope we make it in time, Mom. Twitchy hasn't eaten anything since I found her over a week ago!"

Mom looked at me, concerned. I'm sure she was thinking the same thing I was... hoping that Twitchy won't die on the way there. Twitchy certainly wasn't as active as she had been days earlier, and now being in such a tiny, empty jar with nothing natural to stand on couldn't have been much fun for her.

With Twitchy's little jar on my lap, we sat in silence for the next half hour as the traffic jam sputtered along. I checked the dashboard clock. Four thirty-five!

The skyscrapers of Philadelphia were in plain sight on the horizon, and traffic finally seemed to move a little faster. Mom stepped on the gas, changed lanes, and carefully passed slow moving cars several times; determined to get Twitchy and me to the museum on time.

Mom handed me her phone.

"Call the museum and tell them we're on our way."

I dialed, and when the receptionist answered, I asked her to tell Dr Alito that we were stuck in traffic, but would be there shortly. I switched off the phone and hoped that my words would be true.

Mom was as focused as ever when we finally exited I-95 and took the ramp into the city. I checked the clock; four forty-five!

"We're almost there, Twitchy!" I looked at Mom and she smiled back.

I marveled at the sight of so many tall buildings crammed into so few city blocks. It felt like we were driving through a canyon!

Traffic in the city wasn't quite as bad as it was back on the highway, but then we had to deal with pedestrians and traffic lights at every block. It seemed like the traffic lights turned red just as our car approached the intersections. I tried not to lose hope.

A few more turns, then onto Franklin Parkway,

and on up to Logan Circle... and there it was; The Philadelphia Academy of Natural Sciences! You couldn't miss it by the dinosaur statues out front.

I checked the clock and it was four fifty-five! Five minutes to closing. Perfect timing!

Mom had no time to find a parking space. She looped around Logan Circle, turned onto 19th Street to the left of the museum, and pulled over to the curb in a no-parking zone.

"I'm staying with the car, Dev. You can get out here. It looks like the side entrance is right there. I'll watch until you're safely inside."

I got out, clutching the jar, and crossed the sidewalk toward the entrance. Mom called out from the car's open window.

"If I'm not here when you come out, don't worry. Just wait by the door until I drive back around the block again."

I waved without looking back, concerned only with getting Twitchy safely inside the museum.

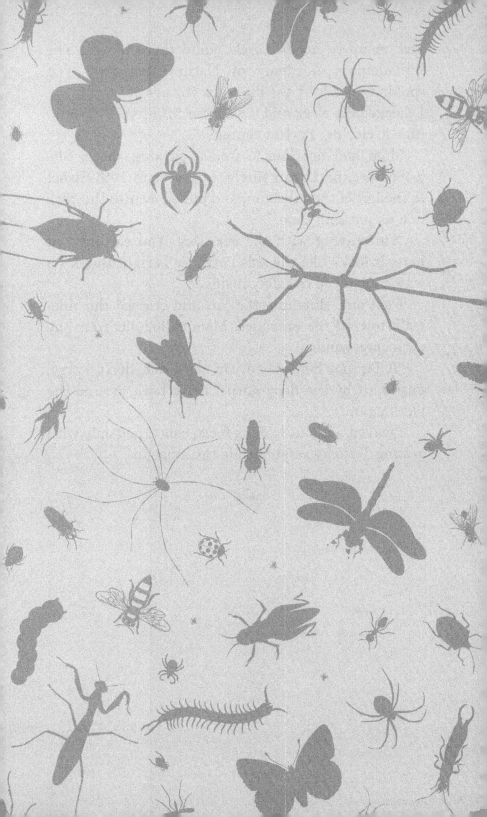

Chapter 24
SHARDS

When I entered the lobby, the place was packed with noisy, rowdy kids and their parents coming out of the exhibit galleries and gift shop as the museum prepared for closing. I approached the front desk, and proudly placed Twitchy's jar onto the counter. The receptionist turned to me.

"Hi, my name is Devin, and I'm here to see Dr. Alito. He's expecting me."

"Ah, so *you're* Bug Boy! I'll call up there to let him know you're here. You can have a seat over there and wait if you'd like."

I breathed a deep sigh of relief, content that I made it in time, and that Twitchy would finally be in good hands. As I turned from the counter to admire the expanse of the commotion-filled lobby, my elbow swung and bumped the jar. To my horror, it flew off the counter and struck the tile floor, shattering into pieces! I stood there, stunned for a moment, as my eyes took in the lid and broken shards of glass, splayed out in a wide field of wreckage across the lobby floor.

"NOBODY MOVE," I screamed at the top of my lungs, and reflexively spread my arms out wide to act as a barrier to keep the kids away from the crash site.

The place instantly quieted down, as if I had yelled, *"FIRE!"*

I bent down and desperately scanned the floor for Twitchy, who happened to be similar in color to the lobby's tile floor, which made it nearly impossible to see her. Honestly, I fought the urge to cry. I scrambled to pick up as many glass shards as I could, hoping not to find a crushed Dryinidae wasp among them, or allow time for her to end up under some kid's shoe!

Then she suddenly appeared, completely fine, walking among the jar's broken pieces as if nothing had happened.

"Twitchy, you are one tough little creature!"

I offered her the tip of my finger, just as I had when we first met at my mailbox a week earlier. And just as then, she crawled up onto my finger like we were familiar friends.

The receptionist saw the entire episode and came around with a wastebasket to pick up the glass shards I had collected and brushed off to one side of the front desk. I held Twitchy up in front of my face for her to see.

"Would you happen to have some type of container for my bug?"

"I sure do," she said and went behind the counter. A moment later she produced an empty sandwich container from the lunch she had earlier that day.

"This should work until Dr. Alito comes down."

I placed Twitchy inside, snapped the lid shut, and placed the container on the counter... this time *away* from the edge!

A few minutes later, Ron entered the lobby.

"Hi Devin, nice to see you again," he said as he shook my hand.

"You too, Ron! You won't believe what just happened!"

I briefly explained the day's adventure and near-tragedy, while handing Twitchy over to Ron.

"You've had quite a day. Let's see what we can do with this little wasp," he said. "Thank you so much for all your trouble getting her here. The museum and I really appreciate it!"

"My pleasure, Ron."

We shook hands once more, and I headed for the exit.

"Have a safe trip home," Ron called out behind me.

I exited the building just as Mom pulled up to the curb. Perfect timing! I got in and buckled up. As we pulled away, Mom asked how it went.

"Great, but you won't believe what happened in there!" I told her about the entire episode, and we had a good laugh.

We sat quietly as Mom navigated through the grid of the city, onto the exit ramp, and out onto the highway. I glanced out into the car's side mirror and watched the city get smaller and smaller behind us, as we headed northward home.

I thought about the oddness of that tiny and rare bug, now inside that huge metropolis! What a long, strange trip it had been for her, and what an exciting, educational, and sometimes harrowing journey it had been for me — all within the span of eight days! I felt blessed and proud to have been able to contribute a rare find to the museum.

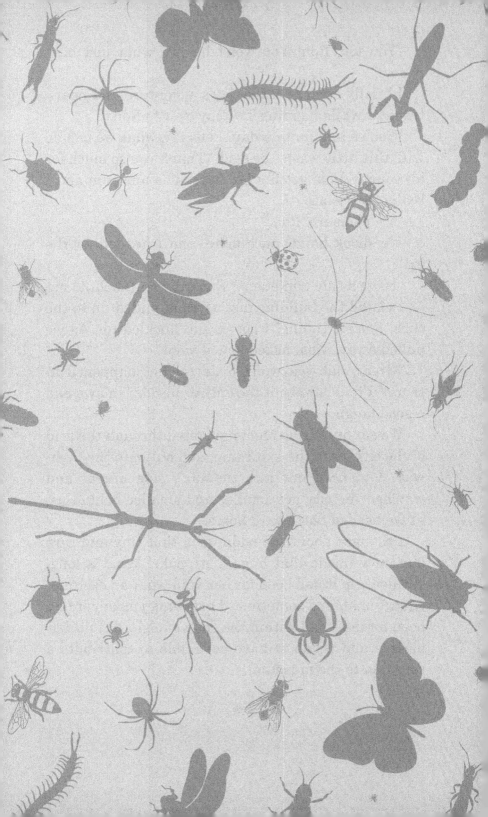

Chapter 25
HOME

Despite the traffic jam going *into* the city, it only took about 20 minutes to get home. Dad had just finished paying the pizza delivery guy who was just pulling away when Mom and I rolled up into the driveway and headed for the garage. I was elated! *Pizza...* a perfect dinner for a perfect day's ending!

We pulled into the garage and Mom went inside to help Dad set the table, while I went out front to collect the day's mail. I approached the mailbox, reached for the lid and momentarily reminisced about the past week, and my little friend.

Bittersweet.

One afternoon a couple of days later, I was in my room finishing my essay on *"The Metamorphosis"* when I heard the phone ring downstairs.

"Devin, telephone! It's Dr. Alito!"

I ran down and Mom handed me the phone.

"Hi Ron! What's up?"

"Good afternoon, Devin! I just wanted to thank you again for your contribution to our collection."

"You're welcome, Ron!"

"Well, I also wanted to inform you that our little friend passed away this morning, but she'll never be forgotten while on permanent display in our vast collection!"

"Aw, I'm sorry to hear that," I replied. "That's life, I guess! But hey, thanks again, Ron. This whole thing has been quite an adventure for me."

"Next time you're in Philly, stop on in to the academy," Ron said. "I'll show you the entire collection, and then some! Have a great day... *Bug Boy!*"

As I hung up, I couldn't help but imagine Twitchy; inside a glass display case, a pin through her thorax, mounted to a board, her Latin name on a tag below, and in the good company of countless other specimens of bug species.

By the way, I got an A+ on my essay of *"The Metamorphosis."* Miss Banks said I have a real talent for writing. Franz Kafka and Miss Banks were my motivation to write this book. And of course, Twitchy was the biggest inspiration of all!

Oh, that *BUG!*

The latter part of this story is based on an actual experience I had as an adult in the early 1990s. Like Devin in the story, I spent many hours as a child, observing and interacting with all types of arthropods in and around our home in southeastern Pennsylvania. I became familiar with virtually every type of insect and arachnid in the region. Even if I didn't know the name of the species, at least I could identify it by its appearance and behavior.

A move to southern New Jersey in my early 20s brought my awareness to just a handful of species I hadn't seen previously, but nothing remarkable or unique... until the day I found a strange little bug on my mailbox. The bug was exactly the one in the story, and like Devin, I had hoped that it was a new species that I could name and take credit for finding. With the help of an entomological collections manager at The Philadelphia Academy of Natural Sciences, I was able to determine that the bug was not a new species, but an extremely rare one at that time.

Other books by Mark C. Collins
- Grandma Stinks!
- Ben's Day
- Meet The Bugs!
- Meet The Bugs! 2
- Harry's Hair
- The Christmas Cookies
- Witch Switch
- Where Did Summer Go?
- Wuff
- My Sun

Website: markcollinsillustration.com

- Mark Collins Illustration
- MCCollinsStudio
- MCCollinsStudio
- mccollinsstudio

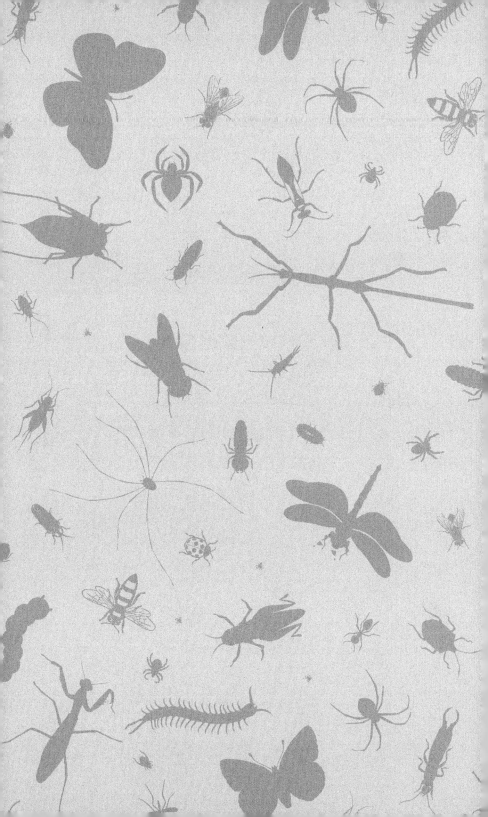

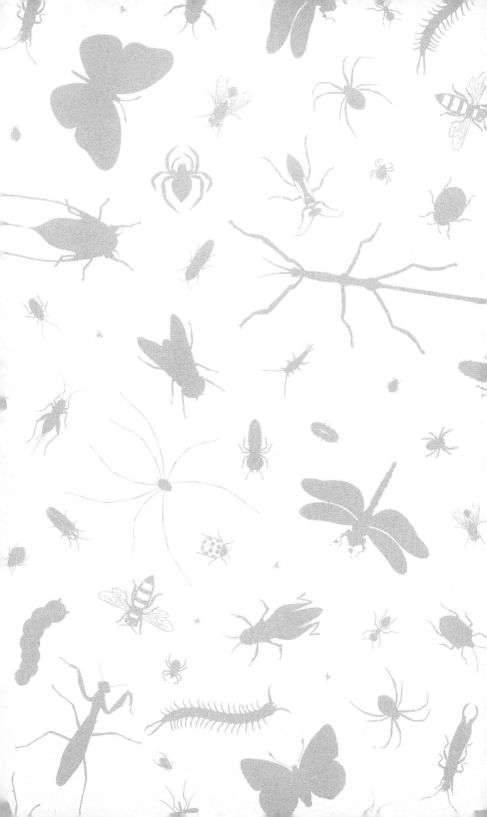